GLIOBLASTOMA, GRIEF *and* GRACE

A Memoir of Our Three Close
Family Members with Glioblastoma

Marcia Collins Jackson

To: CHS
Numbers 6:24
Marcia Jackson
1-22-21

Published by Wheatmark®
2030 East Speedway Boulevard, Suite 106
Tucson, Arizona 85719 USA
www.wheatmark.com

ISBN: 978-1-62787-848-7 (paperback)
ISBN: 978-1-62787-849-4 (ebook)
LCCN: 2020920641

Bulk ordering discounts are available through Wheatmark, Inc. For more information, email orders@wheatmark.com or call 1-888-934-0888.

Acknowledgments

I have been blessed to experience the grace of God in all areas of my life including with family and friends.

Stan Crader, an accomplished author and David's friend for many years, recommended Wheatmark when I asked him about a reputable publisher. Sam Henrie, President and Founder of Wheatmark, offered advice and his expertise when I wasn't sure what questions to ask. Lori Conser, Senior Project Manager at Wheatmark, was very accommodating with design ideas.

My sister-in-law Sue Jackson patiently made editing suggestions and encouraged me to continue. My best friend Kathy Duncan listened to my frustrations with trying to "get it right," and my oldest grandson Alex helped by reading some of the manuscript aloud to me.

The list of credits could be endless but I must mention how grateful I am for having had unconditional love from my parents, for 41 years of marriage to an incredible husband, and for our two daughters and four grandchildren—all gifts from

God. I am thankful for my two sons-in-law, Matt Coomer and Nathaniel Molter. Matt has been so helpful with handyman projects in David's absence and Nathaniel is my pastor and technical support.

Contents

Preface

This book is written in memory of three wonderful human beings—all beloved family members—who suffered from the same terminal disease, Glioblastoma (GBM). I had worked nine years as a RN when my mother-in-law Freda Jackson was the first to be diagnosed with GBM, and I wasn't familiar with this type of malignant brain tumor that is still considered "rare." Nine years after she died, MY mother, Beryl Collins, was diagnosed with this deadly disease. My husband and I were in shock with both our mothers dying from this, and of course they were not biologically related. The attending physicians told us that this is not an inherited disease, and we then considered this a "fluke." I cannot describe the devastation I experienced in 2017 when my best friend and husband of 41 years, David V. Jackson became our third family member to experience hearing his own diagnosis of Glioblastoma, trying to process that he too faced a battle with this aggressive, incurable disease.

One physician described to us that GBM is like sand falling on the brain, making it impossible to completely remove. Another physician used an example of mixing red and blue clay together to make purple, then trying to extract just the blue or just the red. This book is NOT about medical terminology, scientific information or technical information about Glioblastoma. That information can be found online. It is simply our family's story about three Glioblastoma journeys. Some have said that anything that is "shareable is bearable", and there is healing in telling your story. I have found that to be true.

I do not feel sorry for myself because of these tremendous losses because I realize that every person faces their own heartaches, disappointments and struggles. I know that children can also contract this disease and I cannot imagine the sorrow these families face. I do hope to raise awareness of glioblastoma multiforme (GBM) so that risk factors can be researched and eliminated; and to encourage insurance companies to help fund Genetic screening, since it is now believed that certain genetic syndromes can be inherited. (I have read that certain mutated genes may be inherited with GBM.)

Of the three, David was at higher risk with developing GBM since he was male and over the age of 50 (he was 60 when diagnosed). David's mother died at age 63, and my mother died at age 66.

I have tried to find a "common thread" with possible risk factors with our three family members. Is severe emotional trauma a possibility? Freda and David were very traumatized with the death of Verdell, and Mom was heartbroken over her divorce from my father after 23 years of marriage. Does exposure to second-hand smoke or other chemicals increase the risk of the mutation of DNA? Both mothers worked in environments with heavy smokers before public smoking was banned, and David worked as a teen in a car service station with chain smokers and chemical exposure. He was employed as an over the road truck driver, hauling dry bulk products for over seven months before he was diagnosed with GBM. I realize that many people have been in similar situations without developing GBM, and we may never know the answers to these questions.

Our grandson, JJ, now six years old, unexpectedly asked me a few months back, "What did Papa die from"? I stumbled over the right thing to say for his age—and finally said that Papa's brain got "very sick."

In sharing our family's story, it is my desire to offer encouragement to those who are experiencing similar situations with terminal illnesses. With God's grace and the love of family, you will overcome the grief of your great loss and once again find joy in living with a new "normal."

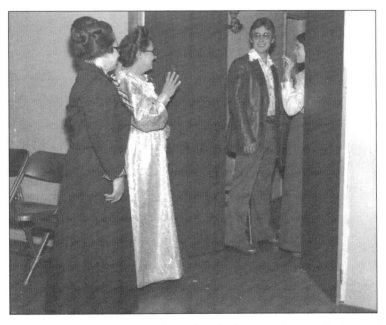

1976 My precious mother and mother-in-law waving to David and me as we left for our honeymoon. Seems surreal that the three on the left were diagnosed with Glioblastoma and are no longer with us.

PART 1

A 13-Month Battle

Early Memories

My earliest memory of my (future) mother-in-law Freda was when I was seven years old and my family was invited to the Jacksons' home for dinner. That's when I recall first meeting David V., who was six years old. He was learning to read and was practicing this new skill with my older sister and me. In later years when we started dating, I teased him that he was trying to impress me then and continued this the rest of his life! Freda and her husband Verdell sang at church services locally and at district events. David's father Verdell and my father J. D. Collins had become friends as ministers, and they had been guest speakers for each other. When Verdell died as a result of a car accident in 1964 at the age of 43, the congregation asked my father to become their pastor. David and his mother were in our church section, so we saw each other often at church events.

Freda later told me that she and Verdell were married 24 years before his death. They were blessed with their second child, David, born more than sixteen years after their only other child, a son named Tom. This special couple had worked closely together at a newspaper *The Banner Press* they jointly owned in Marble Hill, MO, with Tom and his wife Sue. These couples also worked side by side together in ministry, both pastoring churches. Freda was understandably in mourning over the loss of her husband and courageously faced being a single parent, raising David V. who was just seven years old when his dad died. She was grateful for her supportive family, including her parents, her sister and her brother-in-law, who lived nearby. She shared with me that when David heard that his dad had been killed in a car accident, that he said he wanted to die too.

1959 Pictured from left to right: Tom, Freda, and David held by Verdell at Tom's wedding

When our daughter Jill was born, Freda helped us care for her while we were both working. David teased his mom that she allowed Jill to do things she never would have allowed him to do, but we understood that they had a special bond. God and family, especially grandbabies, were most important to Freda.

Scary Diagnosis

Freda routinely kept her annual physical appointments with her family physician, but the last one in 1985 was different. She had felt that "something" wasn't right, but that is the only symptom that I remember her reporting. The doctor ordered a CT Scan and that was when a brain tumor was discovered. Glioblastoma was confirmed when surgery was performed at Barnes Hospital in St Louis, MO. We were told at the time of her surgery that the surgeon could only "debulk" the tumor to prevent damaging other brain cells. (Glioblastoma also intertwines in the brain, making it impossible to completely remove.)

Our second daughter Erica was only nine months old during this time and we struggled to keep a sense of normality while our lives were being turned upside down.

1985 A few months before Freda was diagnosed with GBM. Freda holding Erica; David, Jill.

Radiation Treatments
and Final Days

David drove his mother to her eight weeks of radiation treatments, and he began to observe that she was physically and mentally deteriorating. He was so disturbed by this and told me that he never wanted to go through radiation like this if he was in a similar situation. Tom lived in the St. Louis area at the time and was so helpful with his mother's care on weekends. Freda became more dependent with activities of daily living and two months before she died, she was admitted to a long-term care area of a local hospital. She became progressively paralyzed and passed away in 1986, after fighting a valiant 13 month-long battle. She loved God and her family immeasurably. We deeply felt the loss of her love and support.

June 28, 1986 David celebrating his 29th birthday. His mother died of Glioblastoma less than two months later. She was diagnosed one year earlier.

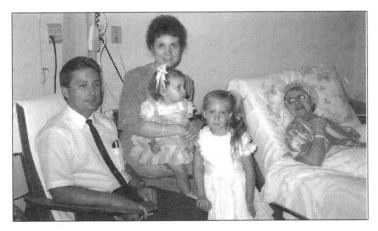

1986 Freda's 63rd and last birthday. David, me holding Erica, Jill; visiting Freda in the long-term care area of the hospital.

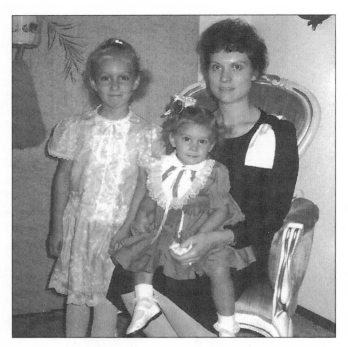

1986 From left to right: Jill, then Erica held by me, before leaving to go to Freda's funeral.

From left to right at the cemetery: Jill; the late Rev. Stanley Chambers, former General Superintendent of the UPCI; David; the late Rev. C. M. Becton, former General Secretary of the UPCI; Tom, former executive administrative assistant to the General Superintendent; and Ken Liley, family friend and funeral director.

1986 Our first Thanksgiving following Freda's death. We decided on eating at a restaurant in St. Louis to be with Tom and Sue.

PART 2

Inoperable

Early Years

My mother Beryl was not yet three years old when her father died from diabetic complications. She was the youngest of five children, and her mother Ruby was left as a single parent with a large farm to run in the small rural town of Hillview, IL. Her ancestry was predominantly German, and her maiden name was Schutz (NOT Schultz). She was an advocate of childhood vaccinations because she didn't receive them and suffered with "whooping cough" (pertussis). Even though she was only about two years old during this illness, she said she could still remember running, just trying to catch her breath with severe coughing.

She excelled in her classes at Coates' one room schoolhouse, a distance of several miles that she walked daily. There was one teacher for Grades one through eight, and Latin was just one of Mom's difficult subjects. She enjoyed school and remembered a time when she cried because she was sick and her mother made her stay home. She was an accomplished pianist and took "the dreaded" piano lessons for 12 years. My maternal grandparents were devoted Christians and their family faithfully attended church. My grandmother Ruby had been a schoolteacher and believed in discipline. She was very serious about proper grammar in her home, and this influenced my mother who made sure that we spoke correctly. Ruby was a superb cook, tended a garden, and served her family organic, healthy meals. My mother was also an accomplished cook and continued the tradition of making sure that we ate well balanced diets.

The one room schoolhouse where Mom attended grades one through eight, many years later in disrepair.

The truck above reads "Schutz
& Sons, Hillview Ill." Inside is Beryl Schutz
and Ruby is standing outside.(1945) The large tree
in the road appears in many photos. It was a local
landmark, in front of Ruby's home.

1945 My maternal grandmother Ruby Schutz and my mother Beryl
Schutz Collins inside the truck when she was about 16 years old.

Mom's schooling was transferred to White Hall, IL High
School after she completed eighth grade. She graduated valedictorian and chose to work for a physician for five years
after graduation. Her job responsibilities included assisting
with medical procedures and helping in the office. She later regretted not taking advantage of her full Nursing School
scholarship, and she stressed to her children the importance of
furthering their education.

Marriage and Moves

My parents met at a church service as teens, but Mom was dating another person at the time. They later reconnected and married when my mother was 23. Soon after they were married, my father Joseph Collins enrolled in Apostolic Bible Institute, St. Paul, MN. This was a long-distance move and the weather was harsh, but they persevered with hard work until Dad's graduation.

Dad's first pastorate was in Doniphan, MO where my older sister Marilyn was born. My parents were then asked to pastor in New Madrid, MO, where I was born when Marilyn was just 16 months old. I teased Mom that I knew I was a surprise, but she would never confirm this. She would always say, "I would never tell one of my children that they weren't wanted"! We knew that we were loved and even though Mom was the major disciplinarian, we were made to feel secure.

My baby brother Mark was born when I was seven years old. Dad was now an evangelist and we were living in Cape

Girardeau, MO. I remember hearing my father talking on the phone when he got the call that Verdell had died in a car accident. The church in Jackson, MO asked Dad to become their new pastor.

1963 Our family pictured with Mom holding my baby brother Mark. Our father is behind my sister and me. I am in the middle, which is fitting since I am the middle child.

The 10 years in Jackson, MO were some of my happiest memories. Mom was a beloved pastor's wife and a stay-at-home mom. Our small hometown was the best place to live and we loved our church, school, and neighbors.

December 1972 Our last formal family picture together. I am in the middle, beside my mother.

1973 My parents and brother Mark at my sister's wedding

Sad Times

My parents divorced and my sister was now married and attending college, and I had started Nursing School. Mom had moved to Cape Girardeau, MO and was a single, working parent to my brother, who was just 11 years old. I admired how she courageously joined the work force once again, after many years. My grandmother Ruby also passed away during this time, but Mom bravely persisted through the sadness and tears. She continued to put God first and her family's needs above her own.

Love of Family

David and I married after I completed Nursing School and became a RN. We moved to St. Paul, MN where David was a student at Apostolic Bible Institute where my Dad had also attended. We made several trips back to MO during the more than two years we lived in MN to help ease my severe homesickness. Of course, we didn't have cell phones then, and I called Mom so much the first snowy winter we spent in St. Paul, that our long-distance phone bill was too expensive to continue to do this. I had to reduce the phone visits to weekends only. We moved back to Marble Hill, MO after our oldest daughter Jill was born. Mom was now a grandmother for the second time (Marilyn's first baby Rachelle was born 10 months earlier) and she enjoyed loving on her grandbabies. She had begun to "find her way" again with a job that she loved, and Mark was there to help her.

Mom was an excellent speaker—she is shown here speaking at our Mother/Daughter banquet at the church we pastored in Marble Hill, MO

Mom's first grandson was Nathan (Ronnie and Marilyn's son); three years later, our daughter Erica was born. All the grand "babies" were so special, and her joy was again increased with the birth of Mark's son Marcus. This was a special time in her life because she had gone through surgery for uterine cancer, followed by breast cancer. She kept Marcus on Thursdays, her day off from work, and she said he was a "bright spot" in a dark time in her life. Mom would hold him and rock him for hours when he was very small. (She would've been thrilled to know that she has a sixth grandchild, Mason, born in 1999. He is Marcus' younger brother and resembles his father Mark.)

November 1995 Mom with grandson Marcus

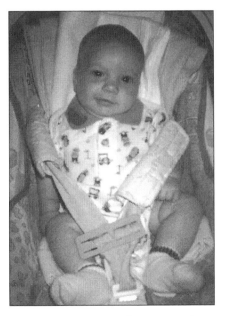

1999 Mason age three months

The summer of 1995, Mom watched Erica (now 11 years old) on Thursdays, while David and I worked. Little did we know just how much we would later treasure these times of bonding with the grandchildren! Rachelle and Nathan lived close-by and visited Mom often. In October of 1995, Mom was keeping Nathan while his parents were attending a church conference out of town. This was also during Nathan's 14th birthday and Mom had a small party for him. His parents were planning a bigger celebration for him when they returned.

1994 Thanksgiving. Mom and her five grandchildren at her house almost exactly a year before her death. (When she learned that she had GBM, she was sad that Marcus would "never remember" her.)

What are the Chances?

Several days after Nathan's party, Mom called and expressed concern about some problems that she was having. She had randomly lost her grip and dropped and broke a coffee cup. Then, when she was driving and started to apply the brake, her foot slipped under the brake instead. Thankfully, she was able to correct this and an accident was prevented. With my nursing background, I began to wonder if she had possibly experienced a "mini" stroke and made an appointment with her family physician as soon as possible. I accompanied her to Dr. Icaza's office, and after performing a neurological exam, he ordered a CT scan. Our family was later called into his office for the results. We were totally unprepared and in disbelief when we heard that our beloved mother had a brain mass, most likely a brain tumor.

After her visit to the neurosurgeon, Mom clung to the hope that maybe the mass was an infection and consented to a brain biopsy that was performed about two weeks after her original CT scan. Unfortunately, the results confirmed GBM. We were stunned to hear glioblastoma again! What were the chances of this happening to both my mother-in-law and my mother?

Numbness, grieving, and extreme sadness cycled many times over with our emotions. We dreaded a second journey with this aggressively terminal disease.

This time the GBM was determined to be inoperable because of the location in the posterior area of the base of her brain. We were told that with radiation, Mom had maybe nine months to a year to live. We were heartbroken but our trust was in God, and with His help and the support of our family, we decided that we would do our best to face this time of distress together.

November 5, 1995 Mom right before her brain biopsy

Radiation Treatments
and Final Days

Mom's condition deteriorated rapidly after her brain biopsy. While we were in the waiting area for maybe the second or third radiation treatment, she began to fall over against me, unable to keep her balance sitting up. We discussed this with the oncologist and the treatments were discontinued. She progressively weakened and was admitted to the hospital during Thanksgiving. I remember my sister and me taking food to her, but she had lost her appetite. She developed blood clots in her lungs (pulmonary emboli) and breathing became difficult. The neurosurgeon explained that Mom couldn't be given blood thinners for the blood clots because of the risk of a brain bleed.

December first, 1995, my mother took her last breath with her family near. It is hard to describe the deluge of tears and depth of sorrow I felt in the loss of my mother who had always been "there" for my siblings and me. I didn't want to face that I could never talk to her again, especially because I always valued her opinions and knew that she "had my back." I had compared her love to a cushion, and now I felt the harshness of the absence of this in "my world." I was so thankful for my husband who loved me and was my best friend, and our two precious daughters, as we helped each other through this very sad time.

December 3, 1995 Youngest granddaughter Erica singing at Mom's funeral. Beryl died from GBM about six weeks after being diagnosed.

PART 3

Didn't See This Coming

Early Years

Verdell and Freda were very surprised when they learned that they were expecting their second baby, since their only other child, Tom, was sixteen. They called David V. their "miracle baby" and they were in for "the time of their life." Tom's personality was more reserved and the quieter of the two. David was more outspoken, very inquisitive and could be quite the challenge! His mother told me that David would take his nice toys apart to see how they were made, and at the time, it was very frustrating. (Later this was a positive thing because he learned to fix basically anything including vehicles, computers, and his airplane.) Tom and Sue married when David was almost two years old, so he was raised as an "only child." He became an uncle at age three when Tom and Sue's son Brad was born; then again at age six when Marcia was born. They became more like friends and playmates because of the closeness in age.

David V. Jackson was definitely his father's son. He followed his dad around and accompanied him as much as possible.

Verdell with David on tractor

Verdell and David napping in the recliner

Verdell had experienced heart problems and had been hospitalized several times in 1964. David ordinarily would've ridden with his father on his way home from work at the Banner Press; but on this Saturday, September 12th, Freda was driving a new car, and David was really "into cars." Providentially, he chose this day to ride with his mother instead. When Verdell didn't arrive home when expected, Freda went to look for him. Verdell was never coming home again. He died from fatal injuries sustained in a car accident. They tried as gently as possible to tell David that his dad had died. As an adult, David faintly remembered running away from everyone and saying that if his dad died, then he also wanted to die.

David later told me that he could remember very little about his father's funeral, thinking that he was self-protecting from the grief. I recall waiting outside in our car at age eight during the visitation at the funeral home, while my father paid his respects to David's family.

David's second grade year was a stressful time, trying to adapt to just a one parent home, and his grieving mother was also trying to cope with this huge loss. He remembered the extreme sadness in their home, as well as with the extended family. His maternal grandparents and his maternal Aunt Lois and Uncle Roy were nearby and helped to fill the void his father left. His brother Tom and Sue moved to St. Louis several years later for a job at the church international headquarters, but they also continued to be supportive and visit when possible.

Church and faith were very important in David's life, and his father had been his pastor. Their church was later blessed with Pastor Howard Brown, also a friend to the family who helped them through this painful time.

Marble Hill, MO was a great place to grow up and everyone helped each other like family. Freda was reassured by a community of family and friends who watched David while she was working. David's maternal grandfather Tom Stevens and his Uncle Roy kept him busy with helping with farm work and mechanical projects. David told me that he got mad at his grandfather when he had to work so hard in the heat, baling hay. He wanted to stop, but Grandpa Tom said they would pause for lunch and then they would work until the job was completed. This work ethic was so ingrained in him and carried all through his adult life. His Uncle Roy would give him things to fix—including an old washing machine that David put back together for him when he was about 11 or 12 years old. Grandpa Tom and Grandma Dorothy lived two houses down from David and his mother after Verdell died. David said that he spent hours on their porch just talking. In one conversation he told his Grandmother that he was going to marry Marcia Collins. I of course did not know this until after we were engaged.

Dating

I was always aware that David V. was around and saw him usually once a month at church sectional services or activities. Freda would drive him to Jackson, at the church my father pastored, to keep him involved in our youth fellowship. I was only interested in him as a friend when we were middle school age, and I tried not to hurt his feelings when he gave me a note to circle yes or no if I liked him? But things began to change when we were teens. I soon noticed how handsome he was, his demeanor, and that he was a talented guitar musician. (Plus, I thought it was "cute" that he had the distinctive trait of being left-handed!) I realized that I was falling in love with him and this time it was more than just a friendship. We would talk for hours, sharing secrets and our lives. We were too young to single date until I was 16, but we double dated at times with my sister Marilyn and (her now husband) Ronnie.

1974 David and me at my home in Jackson, MO during dating years

1970s in Fellowship Hall of Jackson church

We dated about four years total, but we split up for about a year. During this time, I was in Nursing school and David was a student at Apostolic Bible Institute in St. Paul, MN. David called me the summer of 1976 while he was on quartet tour with students from the bible college and we began again as a couple. We became engaged in August. After our engagement, Mom told me about a service that David had attended at our church when he was 11. He had been on the platform and walked by the organ that she was playing while she was praying about my future spouse. She had waited years to tell us this so that she wouldn't influence our decision to marry.

Marriage and a Move

We were married December 18, 1976, and after a honeymoon to Orlando, FL and Disney World, we returned home to celebrate Christmas with our families. New Year's Day, 1977, we moved into an apartment in minus 40 degrees and extreme snowy weather in St. Paul, MN. I battled homesickness during our first six months there, and when I wanted to be back in MO, Mom reminded me that this time would soon pass. I rode a city bus to work as a nurse in a St. Paul hospital since we only had one car.

December 18, 1976 Wedding Day in Cape Girardeau, MO. The temperature was 65 degrees!

Back to MO

We moved back to MO in 1979 after our first baby girl, Jill, was born. David worked at a car dealership and later as an insurance agent. I was employed as a nurse. Freda helped us care for Jill while we were working, and we lived with her while our house was being built in the Gravel Hill (Burfordville) community.

David was elected as pastor of our church in Marble Hill in December of 1982. I played the keyboard and worked closely alongside David as pastor's wife. We loved our congregation and had many great memories there. In 1984, our second baby girl, Erica, was born. Both Jill and Erica developed their singing talents while we served as pastor, and they were very involved and helpful to us in our church.

1984 David was a gifted speaker and teacher. One of his chalk drawings he used to illustrate the lesson.

When Jill was just seven years old, and Erica was not quite two years old, Freda died as a result of GBM. We felt the tremendous impact of the loss of David's mother and the children's paternal Grandmother. She had been a "pillar" of faith at our church and we had relied heavily on her.

1988 Jill in front of me, David holding Erica following church service

At the end of 1988, we moved into Marble Hill on what had been David's grandfather Tom's property for many years. David had excellent carpentry skills and drafted plans to build our house there. We chose (he always said I was the one) to live on the property in a two-story shop he built, so we could be on site during the build. It was supposed to take him about six months, but with working other jobs, it took him about two years. This was an intensive labor of love. He hauled old bricks that he had to manually clean and everything was constructed from "the ground up." Several friends came to help during these hard years including Howard Brown, Craig Mitchell, and Pastor Jim Mahurin.

The finished product. David was a perfectionist!

My husband was also an aviation enthusiast and began his first flying lesson in May of 1989. I was not a fan of his learning to fly, but I finally "got on board" after he made his case to me that he had tried to always support me in my aspirations. I was concerned for his safety, but he said that the more you learn about flying, the more you understand how safe it is. David also reassured me that if something happened to him while flying, remember that he was doing something he enjoyed. He became an instrument rated pilot and flew our family many miles across the country including CO, TX, MI, FL, AL, NE, etc.

David standing beside his plane. He later tackled the huge job of re-painting the aircraft!

David and I enjoyed multiple annual trips to the Oshkosh Fly-In and camped in a tent beside our plane.

July 2012 beside our plane and tent at Oshkosh Fly-In

David V. landing his Piper Cherokee

David passed along his love of animals to his daughters. He taught Jill how to care for her horse Star, and Star delivered a colt Skylar on our property in 1993. We enjoyed watching him grow bigger than Star, and his antics were like therapy!

David knew the importance of connecting with other ministers locally, statewide, and nationally. He was our sectional secretary for 13 years and also served as our sectional Sunday School representative. This allowed him to work closely with Pastor James M. Molter, our state director for Sunday School. In 1989, David was appointed to serve as our MO District Youth Secretary. He held this position for five years and we enjoyed meeting people across the state during ministers' conferences, youth conventions, and church camps.

1992 Preparing to board a plane to General Conference, our annual International Church Conference

1994 Our family at Easter

From 1991 to 1998, David was employed by the city of Marble Hill as City Administrator. This was a demanding job dealing with regulatory compliance issues, supervision of employees, and communicating with the community citizens. He was also in charge of budgeting and payroll, which he computerized while there.

1994 David supervising road repairs while working as City Administrator

In 1998, he was asked to be Safety Director at Black River Electric Cooperative, where he worked until 1999, when he received a call to pastor in Tennessee.

The Line

P.O. Box 31, Fredericktown, M

m

seven years as City Administrator of Marble Hill. Prior to that he was Manager of JW Chevrolet in Marble Hill and the Agent

David Jackson, Safety Director

In the Newsletter while working at Black River Electric Co-Op

Deep Roots

It was difficult for David to leave the home he built on property his grandfather had previously owned; but he knew that God was leading him in this direction, and when he obeyed, our family would be blessed. We were also confident that God was expanding our horizons and influence. Bollinger County had been his home—where he was raised, attended schools, and then pastored. He had spoken at various community events, including Jill's baccalaureate and commencement. He had served as PTA president, on the school curriculum committee, and had driven a school bus.

David speaking at a community event

Tennessee Pastorate

David V. served as a pastor in Hohenwald, TN from 1999–2005. While there, he assembled a prayer group for community ministers and was active in the Civil Air Patrol. I worked as a nurse at a Same Day Surgery Center in Columbia, TN and I was church Music director, along with our daughter Erica. We began summer Vacation Bible School sessions, organized Sunday School bus routes, and encouraged Children's Ministry. We made lifelong friendships and many good memories there.

David built a large shop on our two-acre property in Hohenwald. We enjoyed this beautiful area, just outside of the city, and had great neighbors.

Our home in TN. David built the shop on the right.

David volunteering with the Civil Air Patrol

We were thrilled to celebrate our 25th wedding anniversary with family and friends in December 2001.

The invitation David created for our 25th wedding anniversary celebration. The middle picture is from our wedding day in 1976: David's mom on the left, and my mother on the right

In 2001, our older daughter Jill graduated from MTSU in Murfreesboro and began her studies in Veterinary Medicine at St. George's University on the island of Grenada, West Indies. We accompanied her on her flight to settle in before classes began.

Beautiful campus of St. George's University, Grenada, W.I. before damage by a hurricane

In 2003, our younger daughter Erica graduated as valedictorian from Lewis County High School and began attending college about 30 miles away.

Our family at Erica's high school graduation

Second Family CD Project

We completed our second family gospel music recording CD in 2003, produced by Kevin McManus in Nashville, TN with the Zion Music Group. This was a compilation of 10 songs that I had written, and the project was titled *Go for the Gold*. We were chosen to sing at our General Conference, held that year in Toronto, Ontario, Canada. Jill flew in from Grenada to be with us.

The cover for our Project, Go for the Gold. I composed the song "Go for the Gold" after David preached a sermon about this theme, using the scripture I. Corinthians 9:24. David uploaded the title song "Go for the Gold" on YouTube: Go for the Gold Youtube 960 x 540—YouTube

Singing at Toronto, Ontario, Canada at our General Conference

2003 Missions Trip

In the fall of 2003, David went on a Missions trip with minister friend Bryan Nerren to Thailand and Cambodia. He was forever changed by this enlightening experience and always dreamed of going back to visit this area.

2003 Missions Trip to Thailand and Cambodia

2003 Thailand/ Cambodia Missions Trip—Speaking with an interpreter

Hurricane Ivan on Island of Grenada

Hurricane Ivan caused extensive damage to the Island of Grenada in 2004, while Jill was attending St. George's University there. Flights were cancelled into the country and Jill's only communication at the time was per email. She was able to let us know that she was okay, and several days later she was able to briefly call. Our friend and Missionary Carlton Jackson, who was in the U.S. at the time of the hurricane, called David to ask him to meet him in FL and fly with him on a humanitarian trip to Grenada. They were miraculously allowed to board a plane at Trinidad, and David was able to help Jill leave the island several days later and fly to Puerto Rico, where the power was also out from the hurricane. The next day they were able to fly home to await a decision on a location where veterinary classes would continue. Jill's class was then moved to Purdue University, West Lafayette, IN to finish the semester there, while the Island campus was being repaired.

David, right front, helping assist Missionary Carlton Jackson and a team with Mark Majors in response to Hurricane Ivan

Erica was now attending Indiana Bible College in India-napolis, so we picked her up on our way to celebrate Thanks-giving 2004 with Jill.

Sharing a Thanksgiving meal, that I had prepared, with others from St. George's University, displaced to West Lafayette, IN. Purdue was gener-ous to open their campus to them. David pictured in the middle, Jill on the right.

There were also some very difficult times while pastoring in TN. David bravely faced disappointments and opposition from some congregational church "leaders" but continued to do what he knew that God had called him to do. He would reassure our family that there were lessons to be learned with these experiences—remember NOT to follow the wrong ex-amples of people refusing to relinquish total control of church finances and decision making.

In spite of the negatives, David was happiest and fulfilled when pastoring and ministering to others. He was gifted as a teacher in simplifying concepts. He was also creative with photography, one of the ways he used to connect with people and capture life's random, special moments. He mentioned several times that at the end of his life, he desired to receive a "shepherd's crown" (a pastor's reward) in heaven.

Grenada Missions Booth, Salt Lake City

What an honor to be able to travel with Missionary Carlton Jackson to the field of their calling in the aftermath of Hurricane Ivan to deliver food, water and medicine to the United Pentecostal Pastors and churches on the Island of Grenada.

Special Thanks...

Special thanks to the following organizations and individuals for voluntary and immediate responce with emergency assistance to send Pastor Jackson to Grenada to bring hurricane relief.
- Eddy Duncan Family

General Conference 2004 in Salt Lake City, Utah, was a tremendous blessing with more that 50 persons being baptized in the lovely name of Jesus Christ and 202 receiving the baptism of the Holy Spirit as evidenced by speaking in other tongues as the spirit of the Lord give utterance.

Prayer Requests...

30

Days of Prayer & Fasting

OCTOBER 2-31

2004 A sample of many church bulletins David made weekly for our church. Carlton and Dana Jackson are pictured to the right of David and me at one of our GCs that was held that year in Salt Lake City, UT.

Promotion and Move to
St. Charles, MO

In August of 2005, David received a phone call to become the Executive Administrative Assistant to our General Superintendent, Rev. Kenneth Haney. This promotion required a move to our church headquarters in St. Louis. Jill was in Grenada and Erica later joined us after completing her semester of college.

David's many job responsibilities included: managing budgets, coordinating General Conferences, and oversight of the building tours. He also produced the annual presentations of Order of the Faith, a yearly ceremony to honor ministers chosen for their efforts in promoting God's kingdom. I worked part time in Ladies Ministries and I also assisted David with registration for GC. Later I was asked to work in the Stewardship Department and continued to assist David with GC registration.

December 2005 David setting up his office

2006 Trip to Azusa St. in Los Angeles, CA with the Haneys and other leaders from our church headquarters

Dr. Jill's Veterinary Medicine Graduation

Jill graduated from St. George's University School of Veterinary Medicine in June, 2007. The graduation was held in Radio City Music Hall, New York City. Our family, including Tom and Sue, was present for the ceremony to celebrate this great accomplishment. With God's help, Dr. Jill pushed through the grueling, more than nine years of study to become a veterinarian. She credits her dad with helping her understand some of the technical skills she needed to learn with performing surgery. Even though David wasn't medically trained, he was brilliant and mechanically gifted.

Our family attending Jill's veterinary medicine graduation

Later that year, we accompanied Dr. Jill to Las Vegas, NV for the Educational Commission for Foreign Veterinary Graduates (ECFVG) exam mandated for her to practice in the U.S. This required several days to complete, and we were so excited when she got her passing results.

At Hoover Dam, enjoying some sight-seeing breaks during Jill's exam

Animal Love

Dr. Jill rescued a puppy she named Piper and we all became very attached to him, especially David. Jill trained Piper to recognize about 60 words, and one of the words he recognized was "Jackson." When we would call Jill to tell her that we were on our way for a visit, she would tell Piper that Jackson and Marcia were coming. He would run to the door and whine. David took Piper for walks and would spend a lot of time playing fetch with him.

Visiting Piper—he always wanted to play!

Several years later, Jill rescued Prisca, a Jack Russell Terrier, who tried to take over as boss! They liked to visit us in St. Charles.

Erica also wanted a pet, and David consented to a cat because we were living in St. Charles with limited yard space. A friend was getting married and needed to rehome her calico cat, Phoebe, Erica's first cat. A year later, David accompanied Erica to an animal shelter and encouraged her to bring home a sweet, black cat that he picked out for her. Erica named her Pasha, and Pasha also adored David. She would rub his shoes and loved his attention.

David spending play time with the cats. David watched out for Pasha because Phoebe didn't play well with others!

David chose to create family newsletters instead of Christmas cards for several years, journaling our family experiences.

CHRISTMAS 2008

the Jacksons

Dear Family and Friends,
As we celebrate Christmas, we deliberately focus on the many blessings each year brings, and 2008 was exceptional. We especially want to acknowledge that all our good gifts come from God, and that, with Him, all things work together for good.

In January, Jill began working at the Veterinary Clinic of the Mineral Area in Farmington, Missouri, where she is now a fully licensed veterinarian. We were sad that this required "Dr. Jill" and our "grand dog" Piper to move. Piper was our very first house pet and he became part of our family. Thankfully the distance between us is only a one and one half hour drive (30 minutes by air) and we can visit more often.

Our loneliness was soon lessened when Erica's adopted cat Phoebe came to live with us about 2 weeks later. She's made herself at home and loves everyone in her family except for Piper. I can't seem to make her understand that Piper lived here first.

Also in January David and I were privileged to attend for the first time, the "Landmark" conference in Stockton, California. We were so uplifted with the awesome spiritual atmosphere in each service, and experienced prayers answered there.

Erica began her new job as administrative finance secretary in the General Youth Division at our headquarters in April. She continues her college classes fulltime and is scheduled to finish her Bachelor's degree next year. Erica also is directing the Youth Music at her church on Wednesday evenings, as well as being actively involved in singing.

We traveled with Jill to Las Vegas in May for her international student clinical, 3 day test, for veterinary licensure. David, Erica and I enjoyed the brief "vacation" while Jill endured the grueling exam. Erica took her first helicopter ride there and announced that she someday wants to be a helicopter pilot. I definitely tried to discourage that idea as I emphatically pointed out the danger involved. (David seemed to enjoy the idea that one of his daughters was interested in being a pilot!)

The week following our trip to Las Vegas, David flew me to Tennessee, for my major surgery at the center where I had previously worked for almost 6 years. I was given the ultimate care by my previous coworkers, and healed quickly. Our great friends Eddy and Kathy Duncan provided us our own "suite" until I was well enough for David to fly me home 2 days later. I was able to return to my part time job in the Ladies Ministries Division about 3 weeks later.

We spent over a week in October this year working at our General Conference in Greensboro, North Carolina. We had the opportunity to attend some of the tremendous services and meet with old friends.

David stays very busy as Bro. Haney's assistant, but he makes time for his "therapy" with flying. His most recent focus during any spare time is working on his plane to increase the speed. He passed the complicated instrument rating written exam in November.

We pray God's blessings on you and your families in 2009.

Love, David, Marcia, Jill and Erica

Happy New Year!

2008 Our Christmas Newsletter

Erica's New Position

Erica completed her Bachelor of Arts degree in Social Science from Ashford University in 2009. She was also employed at our church headquarters, working fulltime in the General Youth Department. She began her position as Music director at the church in Farmington, MO on weekends in the fall of 2009, upon the request of Pastor James M. Molter. Dr. Jill was an associate veterinarian in Farmington at the same time, and David and I visited as much as possible on weekends to see both our daughters and attend church with them.

2010 The late Pastor James M. Molter teased our girls by jumping in the middle while David was taking the photo

Erica and Pastor Molter's son Nathaniel began dating in early 2010. Tragedy struck in June of 2010 when Pastor Molter died unexpectedly of a heart attack. We, along with the congregation, mourned the loss of this great man. He had been a great minister, and he and his wife Barbara were our longtime friends. Nathaniel was then elected as pastor and David was asked to be a part of the ministry team, as we continued to attend church there on weekends. David was always looking for a reason to fly, and he often flew us from St. Charles to the Farmington airport where we then drove the courtesy car to church.

Erica and Nathaniel's Wedding

David was honored to perform Erica and Nathaniel's marriage ceremony at Long Memorial Hall, Farmington, on February 12, 2011. We were blessed with a beautiful day to celebrate this joyous occasion.

David escorting Erica down the aisle to "give her away" and then perform the ceremony

Our family with our new son-in-law Nathaniel Molter

Our daughter, Erica, was now our pastor's wife! She persisted through some difficult subjects and completed her Master of Business Administration degree from Ashford University in July of that year.

Work Travel

David and I were blessed to attend yearly Religious Conference Management Association conferences. At the IL 2010 Rejuvenate conference for meeting planners, David was named planner of the year.

2011 Attending the Religious Conference Management Association in Tampa, FL.

David worked with the late Rev. Haney for four years, then a new superintendent was voted in. David remained at our church headquarters for three more years until his job ended in 2013 with a "restructuring." David was left scrambling to find employment and worked for an insurance company and drove a school bus in the St. Charles area. He maintained his life of integrity through these difficult times. More than a year later, he was asked to return to headquarters in a different position. He prayerfully considered this offer but made the decision to remain where he was already employed.

David with the late Rev. Kenneth Haney at General Conference

I started working as a substitute school nurse and substitute schoolteacher. We began to pray about the next steps we should take for our future.

2012 General Conference, St. Louis, MO

Jill and Matt's Wedding

Dr. Jill and Matt began dating in 2012 and were married on March 23, 2013 in Destin, FL by the beach. David escorted Jill down "the aisle" in the pavilion and performed the beautiful ceremony during an intermittent rainstorm. We gained our oldest grandson Alex, then seven years old. We loved him dearly from the moment that we met him while Jill and Matt were dating. We started a tradition of competing with Alex over who could say, "Love you more than infinity, XYZ and beyond" first! Jill and Matt's new home was in Dothan, AL now, where Matt had served in the military. We were so sad that Alex lived so far away. I would (kind of) tease them that they could choose to live wherever, but Alex needed to live close to us! David kept reminding me that he would fly us as often as possible to AL.

David escorting Jill, and Alex was ringbearer

David performing the ceremony

Nephews Marcus and Mason; Nathaniel, Erica, my brother Mark; Matt, David, Jill, Alex and me after the ceremony

2014 "Papa" David and Alex shared a love of flying

A Big Year

We were so excited to become grandparents two more times in 2014. James Jackson Molter (JJ) was born March 18th to Erica and Nathaniel. Photographer "Papa" and JJ's Aunt Andrea (Nathaniel's sister) couldn't seem to stop capturing every expression or every movement he made. David and I were totally in love with this grandbaby and "Papa" would tell everyone that JJ was "kind of a big deal"!

Papa and James Jackson (JJ) napping

August 31, 2014 Following JJ's baby dedication

Jill, Matt and Alex came in March to meet JJ. Several weeks later they were surprised to learn that they were expecting a baby in November. On October 31st in St. Charles, I had just started handing out candy, when we got a phone call that Jill and Matt were heading to the Hospital because Jill was in labor, more than two weeks early. We packed as quickly as possible, headed to the Fredericktown Airport where David now kept our plane, and began our flight to AL. We were blessed to have a great tailwind and made the trip in just over three hours, shortly after midnight. I kept checking the time during the flight, hoping our new granddaughter would be born on November first. Our granddaughter Callie Dae was born later that morning and we were immediately in love with this little beauty.

"GramMar" and Papa holding newborn Callie

Another Move

We began the process of moving to Farmington in December 2014. We closed on the sale of our house in St. Charles in March of 2015. David began working for the Farmington School District in maintenance and as a bus driver. I started working as a substitute nurse, and then as a substitute teacher.

Love of Family

Our days were brightened with spending time with JJ, and we looked forward to FaceTime and visits in person with Alex and Callie.

2015 Easter visiting with Jill, Matt and our AL grandbabies

2015 Callie's baby dedication

Timeline in Photo Gallery

July 2015 Coomers visiting and family photo op at church

July 2015 Papa and Alex at Ft. Davidson State Historic Site, MO State Park

August 2015 Papa and JJ. We played a "game" with JJ; I would say he was my buddy, then David would say, "No, Papa's buddy"!

September 2015 with Papa holding JJ in the hangar

December 2015 following Christmas church program

March 2016 Papa feeding Callie
during her family's visit

June 25, 2016 JJ's first plane ride with Papa, accompanied by his parents

On David's 59th, June birthday, 2016, he chose to celebrate with flying us to Lambert's Cafe in Sikeston, MO. We had good memories over the years with David flying our family there. We would land at the Sikeston airport, then call for Lambert's courtesy transportation. They would escort us into the Cafe with no waiting, we would eat, and then we would be driven back to the airport.

After flying back home on this day, I told David that it was his day to spend as he desired. He wanted to do a road trip and he drove us to random areas that he said he hadn't been to for some time. We could never have imagined that this perfect day would be his last birthday before brain surgery the following year.

June 2016 David's last birthday at Lambert's

June 2016 David officiated at a funeral of a childhood friend in June 2016

July 2016 Papa holding Callie, after flying Alex back to AL from a MO visit for church camp

Job Change

David continued to work for the school system year-round and assisted with the ministry team at church. He played guitar and sang with his beautiful tenor voice in our church Ensemble. Of course, I teased him that his favorite "fix" was flying and working on our airplane.

With God's help and David's good stewardship practices, we were debt free. Always the visionary, David wanted to build us a retirement home, and saved for this. He wanted to remain debt free and chose to begin driving a semi-truck in October 2016.

October 2016 Random Fly Date Selfie

November 2016 David flew us to Callie's second birthday celebration in AL

David came home one afternoon in November and told me about an incident that had "never happened before." He had tripped and fallen while working on a project in the hangar. He was always careful to practice safety to prevent injury and was intentional in teaching us to be cautious. It seemed insignificant at the time, but in retrospect, I wondered if this was an early symptom of GBM with muscle weakness. He had been complaining of numbness in his fingers and legs and was doing stretching exercises to improve circulation.

Last Christmas

December 2016 Our last Christmas photo together at JJ's house

During December, David filled out the paperwork to qualify for benefits with his job at Beelman Truck Company. He stood at the peninsula in the kitchen and said that he was going to take advantage of every benefit that he qualified to receive after the required waiting period.

40th Wedding Anniversary

On December 18, 2016, David and I were married 40 years. Erica encouraged us to officially celebrate this occasion with family and friends at our church and organized the event. We set the date for December 30th so that Jill's family could be there from AL and we prayed for good weather. We had a wonderful time and our prayers for good weather were answered. Looking back, we noticed that David was repeating himself, which was totally out of character for him.

After all the work, Erica said that the next time she organized and worked that hard to celebrate our anniversary, it would be the 50th! Later we would realize how important this celebration would be forever!

Church sign announcing our 40th Wedding Anniversary celebration

Our family photo during our 40th celebration

Our family together, the day after the celebration. Callie's face is par-
tially hidden behind a cup on the table. (In reviewing this photo later, I
noticed a change in David's smile.)

We Didn't See This Coming

In January 2017, David was getting home late in the eve-ning, then back up early in the morning to drive a truck. He was getting less than six hours of sleep at night, so I wasn't concerned when one evening he told me that he had a head-ache that never went away. He had always had sinus issues for years and experienced headaches randomly.

The following month, I began working part-time as a RN performing health screenings at Parkland Health Mart Pharmacy in Fredericktown, MO. One Saturday while doing screenings at a community event, David came to meet me for a lunch break. He was very tired, and I noticed that he took longer to get ready to meet me there, but again, I knew that he wasn't getting enough rest.

Around the end of April, David said that he was sleepier than usual, requiring him to pull off the road and sleep at frequent intervals. Also during this time, I was surprised to hear David say, "If this is depression, it's awful"! He was un-characteristically so tired and lacked the energy to enjoy being active.

Then in early May, I was worried about him when I saw

his iPhone laying on the nightstand, knowing how careful he was with important information, especially with his iPhone that he "lived by." I called the truck company and they were able to contact him to let him know that he had left his phone at home. He called me from another person's phone around six in the evening and said he should be home around 10. Instead he arrived home after midnight, and I was so relieved that he made it safely. I had been anxiously waiting and praying, wondering if I should call the company once again.

I was so disappointed when David told me that he was too tired to attend a family reunion with me the next weekend. He said all he wanted to do was stay home and rest. I attended with Erica and Nathaniel and was surprised that David was still in bed when I came home that evening.

Monday, May 15th, David called me from his truck. He said he had fallen asleep for about an hour while still parked in the company parking lot and hadn't even left to get the truck loaded. Shortly after his call, the Beelman supervisor called me, concerned about David's behavior and thought he was very pale. He thought he needed a medical evaluation and didn't think it was safe for him to drive. Erica drove me to pick up David. I took him to eat at a local restaurant, and then drove him home. He seemed fine the rest of the evening, and since he didn't have a history of underlying health issues, I decided to wait until the next day to make a medical appointment for him. The next morning, I had an early morning meeting at the pharmacy. David was already up when I got up to get ready. He mentioned about kids coming in and they were going to be "noisy." I then became concerned because I realized that something was wrong and wondered if he had experienced a "light stroke." After he was up longer, he totally improved with no further confusion, so I attended my short meeting. (The physician explained to us later that his confusion most likely improved because once he was up for a while, the brain swelling would decrease because of changing into an upright position.) I told my supervisor about David's symptoms and that I needed to make him an appointment. She advised that I just take him to the Emergency Room, and I agreed. I called him on my way to pick him up, and I told him to be ready to go to the ER when I got there. He said okay, but when I got home, he was still in bed. I helped him get up and get ready, then headed to St. Francis Medical Center in Cape Girardeau, where I had worked years before.

On the way, I called my sister Marilyn and my brother-in-law Ronnie who live in Jackson, MO, (a short distance from Cape Girardeau) to ask them to meet us in the ER. The attending physician ordered blood work, which was normal, then ordered a CT scan of the brain. Shortly after David returned from this, the doctor came into the room with shocking news that David had a brain tumor in the right frontal lobe, already encroaching on the left side. I immediately excused myself while starting to sob, not wanting David to witness this. Ronnie and Marilyn stayed with David while I tried to gain my composure. I never would have imagined that I would hear a brain tumor diagnosis again with my family, and my heart was breaking. Instinctively I knew that we were facing another GBM journey and I didn't think I could bear this again. After all, we were told that this isn't hereditary, right?

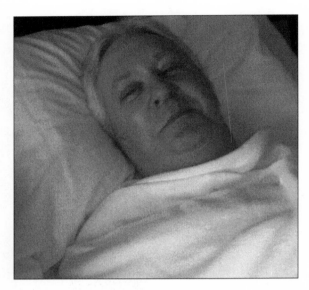

My hero, trying to smile, after his brain tumor diagnosis at St. Francis. In one way, he was relieved to find out what was wrong—but sadly, we were too familiar with these alarming words.

A consulting neurologist came that evening to give us options for treatment. We knew that God had sent him because he was there on a travel rotation to different hospitals, and he was scheduled to leave the next day. He had connections with neurosurgeons at Barnes Hospital in St. Louis, MO, and was able to begin the process for David to be seen by Dr. Zipfel there.

May 19, 2017 Our "babies" with us to David's first appointment with Dr. Zipfel at Barnes. Dr. Zipfel remarked that David was "high functioning." David always pushed to be his best and it was difficult to tell immediately how severe his condition was.

The earliest David could be scheduled for surgery was May 31st, so David and I chose to go home and enjoy our time there as much as possible. I was now the designated driver to avoid any risk of an accident because he was high risk for seizures. He was placed on Dexamethasone and Keppra for brain swelling and prevention of seizures.

During this treasured time together, we discussed our blessed life that we had shared together and just talked about "anything." I admired how David remained calm while facing a very risky procedure with an incurable disease diagnosis, while he maintained that he had had a good life. I marveled that he unselfishly told me that he hated this for me, when he was the one who was suffering from GBM. I tried to hide my random crying, while trying to be supportive. It was emotionally very difficult for me during this time, and I apologized to him for crying so much. He said that this showed that he was loved. He also said that he knew me well enough to know that after I cried, that I would always get up and do the right thing. One day I suddenly burst into tears! David wrapped me in his arms and asked me what was wrong? I told him that I was sad to face the uncertainty of a future without him. He said, "I'm not going anywhere until God says I am"! One of his favorite quotes over the years was, "The steps of a good man are ordered by the Lord...", Psalm 37:23. He also often reminded our family that it rains, "...on the just and on the unjust." (Matthew 5:45)

May 20, 2017 Last time for Papa to be with all the grandbabies before brain surgery

May 21, 2017 After church at a restaurant with family, five days after the shock of learning that David had a brain tumor. He bravely faced this sad news with dignity and class.

May 26, 2017 David's family came to take us to eat before David's surgery. From left to right: David; David's brother, Tom; Tom's wife, Sue; our grandson, JJ; me; David's niece, Marcia; and her husband, Ron.

Brain Surgery

Surgery day, May 31st, we were surrounded by love, prayers, and support of family and friends. Jill had flown in with gifted flight miles from my sister and my nephew Nathan. This was a long day emotionally and physically, and I continued to experience extreme sadness with so many mental (what I termed) "mini funerals." The surgeon gently explained that the tumor was "aggressive" (later confirming a GBM diagnosis). When I began to process the word "aggressive", I hurried out of the consultation area like a wounded animal and started to "collapse" in inconsolable tears. I had to allow myself time to grieve alone, with the realization that my life as I had known it was never going to be the same—I would have to be the caregiver, decision maker, and so much more. Even surrounded by family and friends, I had never felt so alone.

June 2, 2017 David with Dr. Zipfel, two days postop

Back Home

The first two weeks postop at home were some of the hardest days I have ever endured. The right side of David's head swelled to a monster-like appearance. He resisted taking his medicine and any noise was painful to him. Even when I was at the other end of the house cooking or doing dishes, he complained about the noise. He was so hostile that I felt like there was a stranger in the house, and I was worried that this might be a permanent personality change. I would go outside and cry, or call family and my TN BFF Kathy to help me through this. Thankfully, David was more like his previous self after this painful phase. He later told me that during those first two weeks at home he kept thinking that it would get better, but instead he kept feeling worse. I could "feel" the prayers that so many were praying on our behalf and God sustained me.

On his first postop visit following brain surgery to remove as much of the glioblastoma as safely possible, David asked the neurosurgeon if a positive attitude would help someone live longer? He replied that it makes it more pleasant, but it doesn't extend your life. Sadly, GBM intertwines in the brain, making it impossible to totally remove this aggressive malignancy. When faced with painful circumstances, David's signature motto was, "God has the final say."

We spent approximately five hours with multiple consultations on one of the early postop visits to Barnes. This was exhausting, especially for David, trying to navigate to the different areas of the hospital and absorb all the information presented. I took pages of notes so I could reference the details later; but I was feeling overwhelmed with all the medication regimens, risks and side effects. We were told that David qualified as a candidate for a clinical trial because of his rare tumor genetic "markers" found with testing. He chose not to participate in this study because it required spending six to eight weeks in St. Louis, and serious side effects (including blindness) were possible.

I was told by Dr. Zipfel's nurse, Stephanie, that head swelling is to be expected several weeks after brain surgery. But after the edema continued to increase, I emailed pictures of the severe swelling for her to show to Dr. Zipfel. I then had to drive David back to St. Louis for the Doctor to withdraw fluid with a syringe. David was such a trooper, but he said that this procedure was extremely painful. It was a very temporary fix—within hours, the area filled again. It was explained to us that the tumor from the GBM had invaded one of the four ventricles of the brain, preventing the drainage of the fluid. This procedure was later performed a second time and Dr. Zipfel began considering placing a shunt to help relieve the pressure.

David's 60th Birthday

David's 60th birthday on June 28th was spent quietly at home. He enjoyed the calls he received, especially from his brother Tom and his niece Marcia. I had bought him as many "60" cards as I could find, and I heard him talking about this during his phone calls. His head was still so swollen that I decided not to share pictures of his birthday in this book. I wanted to preserve his honor, and I also didn't want his family, especially his grandchildren, to remember him like this.

Supportive Family and Friends

Family, friends, and church family were so supportive with offering to run errands, bringing food, and calling to check on us. There were times when I felt so mentally drained that I didn't want to talk to anyone. But one evening a longtime friend, (also a Licensed Professional Counselor in Franklin, TN) Dr. Beverly McManus, called to talk to David. (Beverly's husband, Kevin, produced our family CD, and he and David were both pilots and enjoyed sharing flying stories.) She then asked to speak to me, and I was comforted by this special call. Beverly told me that difficult times like we were experiencing can affect you emotionally, mentally, AND spiritually. As a couple, David and I had always tried to keep God at the center of our lives, and our church memories were made together. After the call, David said to me, "Don't be afraid to let people speak into your life." He forever had a pastor's (shepherd's) heart.

Our close friends from TN, Eddy and Kathy Duncan came for a visit on the fourth of July. David enjoyed this time with trusted friends, and it lifted his spirits.

Zika Virus

That summer, we were listening to the news, and the word Glioblastoma caught my attention. It was reported that the Zika virus was showing promising signs in the treatment of GBM, and that FDA approval might be possible within a year. We were cautiously hopeful that this might happen in time to help David. (I haven't heard anything further about FDA approval since that time.)

More Complications

Another complication David experienced several weeks postoperatively was a blood clot in his right leg. This was discovered by a venogram after he suffered severe pain. He was placed on Coumadin for this from then on and had his blood levels checked routinely. We had several visits from home health nurses following hospitalizations.

There was so much paperwork to be filled out for disability benefits, insurance, specialist consults, etc. Stephanie was a God send, as well as Carla, a secretary at Beelman. We were so thankful that God helped us with the timing of David's employment benefits. Short-term and long-term disability required a six-month waiting period and David had been employed over seven months before his brain tumor was detected.

David gradually increased his physical activity. He was determined to mow the lawn and walk around the property. In July during an especially hot day, I heard him yell in the garage. (He had always done all the maintenance on our vehicles and I was preparing to take his SUV to a scheduled inspection.) He had knelt to check the tires and became short of breath. I became concerned, remembering how my mother had developed blood clots to her lungs (pulmonary emboli). Erica helped me drive David to the ER in Farmington. After he was diagnosed with a "Saddle Pulmonary Embolism", the medical staff was amazed that David was so alert and had walked into the ER. This is a life-threatening condition and David was sent by ambulance to Barnes Hospital. I tried to follow in our vehicle, but I couldn't safely keep up with them. David called me from the back of the ambulance at least six times, trying to figure out where I was. He would watch out the window to see which mile marker or exit they passed and keep me informed.

Just as I arrived at Barnes, David called me to tell me that he was in the back area of the ER and directed me how to get there. (He was always the navigator because I am directionally challenged!) The nurse was asking him questions about his medical history. I heard her repeat to David his answer that he wasn't on any medications. His short-term memory was showing signs of being affected by his illness and I became even more hypervigilant (if that was possible!) in supervising his care. It was vital that he continued his medicines to prevent seizures and further brain swelling. He had always "taken care of me" and I was focused on making sure that he was going to be receiving the best care possible.

One of the specialists at Barnes estimated that approximately 70% of David's blood flow was blocked by the massive blood clot to his lung. I stayed with him during his almost two-week hospital stay. While there, a filter was placed in his right leg to help prevent any further blood clots moving to major organs. They also placed a shunt in his brain to relieve as much of the swelling as possible. Again, David continued to be very alert, with only occasional times of forgetting where he was. But he was beginning to show signs of exhaustion from all the procedures, MRIs, and multiple consultations. Before one of the procedures, two nurses came in to ask David to sign a do-not-resuscitate (or a no code or allow natural death) order. I noticed a change in David's expression when they tried to explain to him what the order meant. He had previously been more positive about his diagnosis and we had been praying for a miracle. When David hesitated in making the decision, it was requested that I meet with the doctors and nurses. Our daughters were there to offer their support and I leaned on God to help me through this process. I had the confidence that my husband of 41 years fully trusted me to make the right decisions in all aspects of his care. We had discussed many times that neither of us wanted to linger on life support that would prevent a natural death.

Glioblastoma robbed David of his brilliant cognitive (thinking, reasoning, or remembering, according to Merriam-Webster) ability and it was sad to watch his once amazing computer skills decline. He had always taken care of our personal finances and I began to beg him not to log on to his computer because he had begun to make errors. I tried to be as gentle as possible because he had little to do to pass the time, and I wanted him to always feel needed and valued. I would tell him to wait until he "got well." The evening before my birthday on August 11th, I saw him working on one of his office computers. I was afraid that he was going to get mixed up and make more mistakes, especially because I was trying to manage our responsibilities with my limited computer skills. I felt guilty the next day when he handed me the birthday card that he had made for me on the computer the night before. It was very basic, but I knew that he had worked so hard on this and I understood that this would be the last one that he would ever make for me.

Over the years. First picture: examples of cards David made for me. August 2017 Second picture: inside of last card David made for me

WISHING YOU
A DAZZLING DAY
OF DELICIOUS
DELIGHTS.

HAPPY SIXTY ONE!

You are one amazing
woman...!

8-12-19

Marilyn and Ronnie came to take us out to eat for my birthday. David enjoyed the celebration and visit with family.

My birthday dinner with brother-in-law Ronnie and my sister Marilyn. David's brain swelling had decreased some in this picture, after the shunt procedure in July.

Radiation and Temodar

After both our mothers endured unfavorable side effects from radiation treatments for GBM, David and I "promised" that we wouldn't consent to this type of treatment if we were in a similar situation. We were convinced that the benefits did not outweigh the adverse effects. David changed his mind after the medical team explained that radiation is more targeted and calculated now.

His radiation and chemotherapy began in August. This had been delayed because of the brain swelling and blood clots. He tolerated this fairly, but the cumulative effect caused headaches and zapped his energy. He was able to complete all but the last two treatments. We are unsure if the chemotherapy—Temodar—that I administered simultaneously with his radiation treatments, caused some nausea, or if it was the combination of the two. I would pray over the pills as I gave them to him, and I believe that he tolerated them well because of this.

We had a 40-minute drive, five days a week, for David's radiation treatments in Festus. I arranged his schedule so we could eat lunch on the way, to make these days as pleasant as possible for him.

We practiced a modified social distancing while David was receiving radiation treatments and chemotherapy; thankfully, I was able to take him to church services for shorter amounts of time and tried to monitor his interaction with church family. He needed the encouragement of meeting together where he was loved and respected.

September

L abor Day, 2016 was our final time of everyone being together to celebrate a holiday weekend. Jill's family traveled from AL and Erica's family joined us. David was able to attend the Desloge Fair with us that weekend, and then enjoyed being outside with the grandchildren as they played games in the front yard.

Papa, Callie, and Alex

JJ and Callie racing

In mid-September, I drove David to his Jackson family re-union in Jackson, MO. He was beginning to show signs of weakening and I observed tremors in his hands. His confusion was increasing, and his movements were slowing. My "trained eyes" as a nurse observed the progressive worsening of his symptoms, while I also prayed and hoped for a miracle.

I realized the seriousness of the decline in his condition when I took him to eat a few days later. We were sitting in a booth and when it was time to leave, David couldn't get up from the seat. I hurt my back trying to help him up and had to make the decision that I was no longer able to take him to eat without someone to help me.

I awoke on the night of September 18th and noticed the bathroom light on. I found David confused, sitting in the floor, and unable to get up. I called our son-in-law Nathaniel to come and help us. The next day, I called David's family physician and reported the incident. She advised us to take him to the ER. The attending physician there determined that David had suffered a stroke. David was transported by ambulance to St. Francis in Cape Girardeau, for evaluation in their specialized stroke unit. Upon further imaging and testing, another brain tumor was identified instead of a stroke.

The neurologist consulted with the specialists at Barnes and explained that there was nothing further that could be done for David. My family and I agreed that David would want his last days to be spent in the comfort of his home, and arrangements were made for Hospice. We decided on Serenity Hospice because a dear friend from church, Jenna Firehammer, was a coordinator there and was also training as a chaplain.

Hospice

Idrove David home and was relieved to see that church friends had already started moving furniture to make room for the medical equipment needed. David was sleeping more and was especially tired from the trip.

The first week home, family and friends came for short visits and helped by bringing food. Hospice personnel were making visits as needed.

David's brother Tom came to offer support and stayed with David when I needed to run errands. We began to note significant changes in David's mobility with slowed responses.

The second week of Hospice, Jill called, wanting to show David, per Facetime, a presentation she had made for him with pictures and memories over the years. I tried unsuccessfully to help him sit up. This was the first time I observed that he could no longer keep his balance.

Our close friends from TN, Eddy and Kathy Duncan, came to visit two days later, on Friday. David could no longer speak, but he smiled when he saw them. He could blink to communicate, and he now had to be fed. Not long after they left, David started to have difficulty breathing, and Hospice helped set up oxygen for him.

I called Jill and Erica to tell them that their dad's death was imminent. Patti, a special nurse from Hospice, came to help make David comfortable. Erica also came to be with us, but Jill lived about twelve hours away and Facetimed her dad as he was slipping into a coma. She and her family then began the long trip to MO.

During this time of transition, Jenna came and started speaking words of comfort to David and me. God used her to bring calmness and peace in David's final hours.

Sunday morning, October 8th, 2017, (nearly five months after a brain tumor diagnosis) I sang softly to David as he took his last breath and went to heaven to be with Jesus. My heart was broken and anguished with sorrow, but I was thankful that David was now free from suffering and Glioblastoma forever.

Homegoing Service

Longtime family friends Kenneth and Judy Liley, and son, Michael Liley of Liley Funeral Home, directed this special life celebration with their customary distinction. David's extraordinary life was honored with the best anointed speakers and singers. We were blessed with God's presence and love during this special time.

Homegoing Service, October 14, 2017

DAVID V. JACKSON

June 28, 1957 - October 8, 2017

FAMILY PROCESSIONAL...... *"Another Time and Another Place"*

OPENING REMARKS..................... Rev. T.M. Jackson, Brother

SONG .... *"Celebrate Me Home"*
Rev. Craig, Angie and Megan Mitchell

Rev. Scott Graham, MO District Superintendent UPCI

Matt Coomer, Son-in-Law

SONG .... *"Farther Along"*
Dr. Jill Jackson Coomer, Daughter

Rev. Carlton Jackson

Jacksons Singing *"Shackles"* in Grenada, 2002

Rev. Nathaniel Molter, Son-in-Law

SONG .... *"Go for the Gold"*
Erica Jackson Molter, Daughter

MESSAGE.. Rev. Ronnie Brown

DVJ Flying... *"Final Flight"*

Pallbearers
REV. JAY TEAGUE · MARCUS COLLINS · MASON COLLINS · EDDY DUNCAN
KAULIN DUNCAN · RON BOHN · EDDIE BROWERS · BRAD JACKSON

Honorary Pallbearers
TOM SANDERS · PETE SIRDOREUS · JEFF FIREHAMMER
REV. ROGER SKAGGS · REV. NATHAN BROWN

The Homegoing service program

David would have beamed with pride to see the confidence and composure displayed, as our daughters and sons-in-law honored him with their love, respect and treasured memories.

Matt's Tribute

Jill sang "Farther Along"

Nathaniel speaking at the service.

Erica sang "Go for the Gold," the song I composed

Our family, following the service: Coomers, me and Molters. Philippians 1:21, "...to live is Christ, and to die is gain."

I am committed to keeping "Papa's" legacy and memories alive with our grandchildren. We look forward to telling him in heaven about his last grandbeauty, Bethany Arabelle, born in July 2019. She is our "miracle baby," and JJ's little sister. She has brightened our days, and Papa would be once again totally in love with this little gift from God.

Bethany Arabelle Molter

Made in the USA
Coppell, TX
13 January 2021